Give and Take

by Michael Scanlan

Single copies of plays are sold for reading purposes only. The copying or duplicating of a play, or any part of play, by hand or by any other process, is an infringement of the copyright. Such infringement will be vigorously prosecuted.

Baker's Plays
7611 Sunset Blvd.
Los Angeles, CA 90042
bakersplays.com

NOTICE

This book is offered for sale at the price quoted only on the understanding that, if any additional copies of the whole or any part are necessary for its production, such additional copies will be purchased. The attention of all purchasers is directed to the following: this work is fully protected under the copyright laws of the United States of America, the British Commonwealth, including Canada, and all other countries of the Copyright Union. Violations of the Copyright Law are punishable by fine or imprisonment, or both. The copying or duplication of this work or any part of this work, by hand or by any process, is an infringement of the copyright and will be vigorously prosecuted.

This play may not be produced by amateurs or professionals for public or private performance without first submitting application for performing rights. Licensing fees are due on all performances whether for charity or gain, or whether admission is charged or not. Since performance of this play without the payment of the licensing fee renders anybody participating liable to severe penalties imposed by the law, anybody acting in this play should be sure, before doing so, that the licensing fee has been paid. Professional rights, reading rights, radio broadcasting, television and all mechanical rights, etc. are strictly reserved. Application for performing rights should be made directly to BAKER'S PLAYS.

No one shall commit or authorize any act or omission by which the copyright of, or the right to copyright, this play may be impaired. No one shall make any changes in this play for the purpose of production.

Publication of this play does not imply availability for performance. Both amateurs and professionals considering a production are strongly advised in their own interest to apply to Baker's Plays for written permission before starting rehearsals, advertising, or booking a theatre.

Whenever the play is produced, the author's name must be carried in all publicity, advertising and programs. Also, the following notice must appear on all printed programs, "Produced by special arrangement with Baker's Plays."

Licensing fees for GIVE AND TAKE are based on a per performance rate and payable one week in advance of the production.

Please consult the Baker's Plays website at www.bakersplays.com or our current print catalogue for up to date licensing fee information.

Copyright © 1993 by Michael Scanlan
Made in U.S.A.
All rights reserved.

GIVE AND TAKE
ISBN **978-0-87440-899-7**
#185-B

Give and Take was first performed at LaSalle Academy in Providence, RI in November of 1992 with the following cast:

Jennifer Bromley, Amy Colicci, Amy Crooks, Jeff Danielian, Sheila Flanagan, Lauren Gillis, Marybeth Hampton, Maria Ieni, Tanya Izzi, Pat Nugent, Joe Raposa, Angela Rourke, Paul Slade, Mark Tidd, Caroline Trayner, Dan Venditelli, Joshua Willis.

A NOTE ON THE SCRIPT

During the fall of 1992, the students in my acting class at LaSalle Academy in Providence, RI undertook an investigation to see how various cultures responded to the concepts of generosity and greed. We divided the class into continents, and each group was charged to read extensively the folk stories, legends and literature of the various cultures and to select stories which centered around these two concepts. Once we had assembled a representative collection of stories, we then attempted to find a way to dramatize each in a manner which might reflect its particular culture. The result of these efforts is GIVE AND TAKE.

After a great deal of tinkering with the script and adjusting the order of the stories while we toured this piece to schools throughout our state, we arrived at the "final" version which appears in the following pages. However, *our* final version will not necessarily be *your* final version. Please feel free to arrange these stories in whatever order seems to make the most sense for your performers and audience. If you need to delete some of the stories because of time limitations, try to make certain that those which remain include a fair geographical sampling. Also, whatever attempts you can make to present the stories in a style which reflects the culture of origin will be a benefit both to your performers and to the audience.

I hope you enjoy this multi-cultural experience as much as we did!

– Michael Scanlan

GIVE AND TAKE

ACT ONE

(The stage is in darkness. A rattle establishes a steady rhythm, and slowly other instruments are added as the LIGHTS come up. The actors enter and chant (or "rap.")

STORYTELLERS.
The world is immense from west to east --
A multi-cultural banquet, a spectacular feast!
The world's a mosaic, every country a tile
With a particular story, a particular style.
But theres a common thread and a common need –
A well of generosity, a bucket of greed.
No matter where you live,
Make no mistake,
There are people who give
And people who take.
Yes, people who give
And people who take.

(This may be repeated until all are in position for the first story.)

STORYTELLER. A Bantu tale . . .
STORYTELLERS. ANANSI FINDS A FOOL!
ANANSI. Among the Bantu people there was an exceptionally clever young man named Anansi.
ANENE. Among the Bantu people there was an exceptionally lazy and greedy young man named Anansi.
ANANSI. One day Anansi came up with a plan to catch

fish without having to do any of the work. To put his plan into action, he went looking for a fool. Seeing his friend, Anene, he immediately decided that he did not have to look far to find someone dumb enough. "My good friend, Anene, I was just on my way to catch some fish. Would you like to come along?"

ANENE. Anene was immediately suspicious, but decided to play along with Anansi and take this opportunity to teach the scoundrel a lesson. "I'd be delighted to accompany you, old friend. Two can catch more fish than one."

ANANSI. And so they started out towards the river.

ANENE. First, they had to build some fish traps.

ANANSI. So they found some big trees. But before Anansi could suggest it, Anene said . . .

ANENE. "Anansi, I'll cut the branches."

ANANSI. This was going to be easier than he thought.

ANENE. "Yes, I'll cut the branches, and you can get tired for me."

ANANSI. "Wait. Why should I get tired for you?"

ANENE. "Well, when there's work to do, someone has to get tired, right?"

ANANSI. "Yes."

ANENE. "So, it's only fair that if I cut the branches, you get tired, right?"

ANANSI. "Well . . . Oh, no you don't. You can't trick me. I'll cut the branches and you get tired."

ANENE. "But . . . "

ANANSI. "I insist!"

ANENE. "You insist?"

ANANSI. "I certainly do."

ANENE. "Well, in that case . . . go ahead."

ANANSI. So Anansi climbed up the tree and began to

GIVE AND TAKE 7

hack away at the branches.

ANENE. And Anene pretended to grow tired. "Oh . . . Aren't you finished yet? This is exhausting."

ANANSI. "Don't be such a weakling!" But to himself he said, "What a fool."

ANENE. Soon the branches were cut, and Anene said, "Now I get to build the fish trap. It's your turn to get tired."

ANANSI. "Oh, no! You are doing such an excellent job of getting tired that it would be foolish of you to do anything else."

ANENE. "But . . ."

ANANSI. "I insist on making the fish traps."

ANENE. "You insist?"

ANANSI. "I certainly do."

ANENE. "Well, in that case . . . go ahead."

ANANSI. And as Anansi went to work on the fish trap . . .

ANENE. Anene became so exhausted with the effort that . . .

ANANSI. To Anansi's great satisfaction . . .

ANENE. Anene fainted dead away. (*He snores.*)

ANANSI. "What a fool!"

ANENE. Soon the trap was completed, and Anene said, "It's my turn to work now. I'll put the trap in the river, but if a crocodile bites me, you have to die for me."

ANANSI. "Absolutely not! What kind of fool do you take me for? I will put the trap in the river, and if a crocodile attacks, you can die for me!"

ANENE. "But . . ."

ANANSI. "I insist!"

ANENE. "You insist?"

ANANSI. "I certainly do."

ANENE. "Well, in that case . . . go ahead." And Anansi waded into the river to set the trap.

ANANSI. As he waded in, he thought to himself, "What a fool that Anene is to risk his life this way."

ANENE. Fortunately for Anansi, no crocodile attacked, and the trap was soon set.

ANANSI. The next morning, there were three fish in the trap.

ANENE. "Anansi, you take the fish today. I'll take tomorrow's catch."

ANANSI. "Absolutely not! This trap is just starting to work. You take today's fish, and I'll take tomorrow's."

ANENE. "But . . ."

ANANSI. "I insist!"

ANENE. "You insist?"

ANANSI. "I certainly do."

ANENE. "Well, in that case . . . I will take the fish."

ANANSI. "Such a fool!"

ANENE. The next morning, there were six fish in the trap, and Anene said, "Wow, how lucky you are, Anansi, six fish! Here, take them."

ANANSI. "I will not."

ANENE. "You won't?"

ANANSI. "If there were three fish in the trap yesterday, and six today, then tomorrow there will be . . . (*Trying to figure it out.*) many, many fish. You take these, I will wait until tomorrow."

ANENE. "But . . ."

ANANSI. "I insist!"

ANENE. "You insist?"

ANANSI. "I certainly do."

ANENE. "Well, in that case . . . I will take the fish."

ANANSI. (*To the audience.*) I'm almost starting to feel sorry for this poor fool.

ANENE. The next morning, there were no fish in the trap.

ANANSI. "The water has damaged the wood! The trap is in pieces!

ANENE. I will take the trap to market. There will be many people who will wish to buy a trap that has proven so successful in the past."

ANANSI. "How dare you suggest such a thing! You got all those fish, and now you want money from this wonderful trap I built, that I set in place, that I caught so many fish with?"

ANENE. "But . . ."

ANANSI. "I insist on selling this trap!"

ANENE. "You insist?"

ANANSI. "I certainly do, you fool!"

ANENE. "Well, in that case . . . go ahead. Sell it."

ANANSI. And Anansi tried to do just that. He took the broken trap to the marketplace, shouting, "Fish trap for sale! Fabulous fish trap for sale!"

ANENE. Unfortunately, he sold the trap to the chief.

ANANSI. "You'll catch many, many, many fish with this marvelous trap."

ANENE. However, when the chief realized that the trap he bought from Anansi was damaged and beyond repair, he flew into a rage, and punished him by making him wear the fish trap on his head.

ANANSI. "What are you people laughing at? Leave me alone! Anene, kind friend, how did this happen? What did I do to deserve this? Advise me, good friend."

ANENE. "You really want my advice?"

ANANSI. "I insist on having it!"

ANENE. "You insist?"
ANANSI. "I certainly do!"
ANENE. "Well, in that case here it is:"
ANANSI. "Yes?"
ANENE. "If you really want to go fishing with a fool . . ."
ANANSI. "Yes."
ANENE. "Go alone."
STORYTELLERS.

Make no mistake.
There are people who give
And people who take.

A STORYTELLER. From Medieval England . . .
STORYTELLERS. THE PARDONER'S TALE!
UNDERTAKER. (*à la Masterpiece Theatre.*) Many years ago in a small town there lived three youths who were known for their wildness and rough nature. They spent their days lounging in the tavern, drinking, gambling, cursing and spouting such dreadful swears that I dare not repeat them, and chasing women. A thoroughly disreputable lot of dangerous young men. One day as they swilled their swinish fill of wine they heard the distant sound of mournful singing.

Did you ever think when a hearse goes by
That you might be the next to die?
They wrap you up in a big white sheet
And bury you about six feet deep.
All goes well for about a week
And then the casket begins to leak.
The worms crawl in; the worms crawl out.
The worms play pinochle on your snout.

You toss and turn until you're green
Then puss comes out like fresh whipped cream.

YOUTH #1. (*Over the singing.*) Say mates, what's that blighty screeching about?

YOUTH #2. It's enough to put a bloke off his drink, it is.

YOUTH #3. It's that stupid, stumbling undertaker again.

YOUTH #1. Shut up out there, 'fore I give you a blighty beating.

UNDERTAKER. A little respect, I beg of you. A little respect for one who is dead and who was your friend.

YOUTH #2. One of our drinking blokes, is it?

YOUTH #3. A former friend?

UNDERTAKER. Bertram.

YOUTH #1. (*Gathering around the corpse.*) Not me old blighter, Bertie!

YOUTH #2. Me and Bertie tipped many a cup, didn't we?

YOUTH #3. What gone and got the poor boy?

UNDERTAKER. Death. Death in the form of the bubonic plague.

ALL YOUTHS. Poor Bertie. Done in by the Grim Reaper!

YOUTH #1. That blighty blighter death. I'd like to kill him.

YOUTH #2. I'd like to drink death dry, wouldn't I just?

YOUTH #3. I'd thrash and throttle the throat of death if I could get me hands on him.

UNDERTAKER. What an amusing idea. You wish to kill death?

ALL YOUTHS. You bet!

UNDERTAKER. Well, I suppose first you must find him.

YOUTH #1. Where is the blighty scavenger?

YOUTH #2. Where?
YOUTH #3. Where?
UNDERTAKER. Everywhere.
YOUTH #2. Everywhere? Then we might as well start looking in the Tavern, mighten we?
YOUTH #3. Coor, put aside your desire to drink a drop, you drip.
YOUTH #1. If the blighter's everywhere, then everywhere is where we'll blighting well look. (*THEY begin to search "everywhere" for death.*)
UNDERTAKER. Excuse me, gentlemen. I have been told on very good authority that death can often be found beneath that rather forboding oak tree.
YOUTH #1. Thanks, old mate, you ain't such a bad old blighter after all. (*To the others as the UNDERTAKER leaves.*) Awright me blighty buckos, let's sneak up on death nice and quiet like and catch the blighter unawares.
YOUTH #2. But first a cup of wine, don't you think?
YOUTH #3. Nay, you numbskull, it's now or never.
YOUTH #2. But I'm parched, aren't I?
YOUTH #1. The sooner we blast the blighter, the sooner you get your drink, mate.
YOUTH #2. Then let's get to it, why don't we? (*Starts to rush the tree, trips.*)
YOUTH #3. Careful, you clod. (*THEY sneak up to the tree, rushing it at the last moment, and terrifying themselves.*)
ALL YOUTHS. AHHH!
YOUTH #1. Well, mates, if the blighter was here, he's blighty gone.
YOUTH #2. After such a fright, we all need a drop, don't we?
YOUTH #1. Shut up and keep looking. No one over

You toss and turn until you're green
Then puss comes out like fresh whipped cream.

YOUTH #1. (*Over the singing.*) Say mates, what's that blighty screeching about?
YOUTH #2. It's enough to put a bloke off his drink, it is.
YOUTH #3. It's that stupid, stumbling undertaker again.
YOUTH #1. Shut up out there, 'fore I give you a blighty beating.
UNDERTAKER. A little respect, I beg of you. A little respect for one who is dead and who was your friend.
YOUTH #2. One of our drinking blokes, is it?
YOUTH #3. A former friend?
UNDERTAKER. Bertram.
YOUTH #1. (*Gathering around the corpse.*) Not me old blighter, Bertie!
YOUTH #2. Me and Bertie tipped many a cup, didn't we?
YOUTH #3. What gone and got the poor boy?
UNDERTAKER. Death. Death in the form of the bubonic plague.
ALL YOUTHS. Poor Bertie. Done in by the Grim Reaper!
YOUTH #1. That blighty blighter death. I'd like to kill him.
YOUTH #2. I'd like to drink death dry, wouldn't I just?
YOUTH #3. I'd thrash and throttle the throat of death if I could get me hands on him.
UNDERTAKER. What an amusing idea. You wish to kill death?
ALL YOUTHS. You bet!
UNDERTAKER. Well, I suppose first you must find him.
YOUTH #1. Where is the blighty scavenger?

YOUTH #2. Where?

YOUTH #3. Where?

UNDERTAKER. Everywhere.

YOUTH #2. Everywhere? Then we might as well start looking in the Tavern, mighten we?

YOUTH #3. Coor, put aside your desire to drink a drop, you drip.

YOUTH #1. If the blighter's everywhere, then everywhere is where we'll blighting well look. (*THEY begin to search "everywhere" for death.*)

UNDERTAKER. Excuse me, gentlemen. I have been told on very good authority that death can often be found beneath that rather forboding oak tree.

YOUTH #1. Thanks, old mate, you ain't such a bad old blighter after all. (*To the others as the UNDERTAKER leaves.*) Awright me blighty buckos, let's sneak up on death nice and quiet like and catch the blighter unawares.

YOUTH #2. But first a cup of wine, don't you think?

YOUTH #3. Nay, you numbskull, it's now or never.

YOUTH #2. But I'm parched, aren't I?

YOUTH #1. The sooner we blast the blighter, the sooner you get your drink, mate.

YOUTH #2. Then let's get to it, why don't we? (*Starts to rush the tree, trips.*)

YOUTH #3. Careful, you clod. (*THEY sneak up to the tree, rushing it at the last moment, and terrifying themselves.*)

ALL YOUTHS. AHHH!

YOUTH #1. Well, mates, if the blighter was here, he's blighty gone.

YOUTH #2. After such a fright, we all need a drop, don't we?

YOUTH #1. Shut up and keep looking. No one over

here.

YOUTH #2. Nothing over here.

YOUTH #3. Not a thing under this tree but this gallumphing great gob of gold.

YOUTH #1. Gold?

YOUTH #2. Gold?

YOUTH #3. Gold.

ALL YOUTHS. GOLD!!!! (*THEY dive on it and start fighting over it.*)

YOUTH #1. Here, here now. There's enough of the blighty stuff to make us all rich men.

YOUTH #2. I could buy my own tavern, couldn't I?

YOUTH #3. You could buy ten taverns, you dribbling drunkard.

YOUTH #2. Let's do it, then, why don't we? (*YOUTH #1 grabs him as he tries to run.*)

YOUTH #1. Wait, mate. Use your blighting head. This money didn't just fall from the blighty heavens. It belongs to someone. If we go rushing into town, what's to keep some blighty bloke from saying as how the money's his?

YOUTH #3. That's using the old noggin, Ned. We don't dare spend it right away.

YOUTH #2. Not spend it, is it? That's like giving a bloke a bottle of the best and sewing his lips together so he can't drink it, isn't it?

YOUTH #1 We should wait til the blighty night and sneak the gold into our houses and hide it for a while.

YOUTH #2. Wait until night with no food and no wine, is it. Let me just slit me throat and get it over with instead of dying of lack of drink slow like.

YOUTH #3. If it's that important to you, you addled addict – you go to town and get some wine and food. We'll wait here with the glorious gold until your triumphant trek back.

YOUTH #2. I'll be back in two shakes with the wine, won't I? (*Starts to run off.*)

YOUTH #3. And the food, you fool, the food. (*To Youth #1.*) What a dreary drunk, forever droning on about drink.

YOUTH #1. A blighty waste, mate, if you ask me. All this money to a man who will blighty well drink it up in a week.

YOUTH #3. Giving gold to a goon is a grievous mistake.

YOUTH #1. Especially when such blighty blokes as ourselves will lose by it.

YOUTH #3. Not to mention how the man's a security risk, probably merrily prattling on to any mate who'd draw him a drink.

YOUTH #1. A sad case. A blighty sad life, that one has.

YOUTH #3. Perhaps we should help hurry it to an expedient end?

YOUTH #1. You're a blighting genius, you are. (*THEY huddle to plot.*)

YOUTH #2. (*Enters guzzling a bottle of wine.*) Ah, now that's better, isn't it? Imagine them blokes keeping me from me drink, and all the time me thinking they was my friends, wasn't I? And hiding the gold, they say, instead of spending it like a regular bloke would. They don't deserve it, do they? They don't deserve a single coin. But how to keep them from it?

UNDERTAKER. Poison for sale! Deadly, life-sucking poison for sale!

YOUTH #2. Poison, is it? Hey, you, give a bloke some of that poison, won't you?

UNDERTAKER. What do you intend to do with it?

YOUTH #2. Well, I . . . uh . . . I got a bit of a rat problem, don't I? And this is just the thing to kill a couple of rats, isn't it?

UNDERTAKER. It is indeed. But you must be excessively careful. Just a drop of this poison will send any rat, or indeed, any man, into such painful convulsions leading to the most horrifying death imaginable that I am reluctant to sell it.

YOUTH #2. Kill a man, would it?

UNDERTAKER. It would indeed.

YOUTH #2. All right, then, hand it over. (*HE does, the YOUTH pours it into two bottles of wine.*)

UNDERTAKER. My good man, why in the name of heaven are you killing your rats with poisoned wine?

YOUTH #2. Just 'cause their rats, don't mean they don't like a little nip every now and then, now does it?

UNDERTAKER. Indeed. Happy hunting. (*HE exits.*)

YOUTH #2. This'll do it. All that wine, I mean gold, will be mine. (*Walking back.*)

YOUTH #1. Here comes the blighter, get ready.

YOUTH #3. Dagger's drawn.

YOUTH #2. Hey, youse, I brought some wine, didn't I just? (*YOUTHS #1 and #3 attack and kill him.*)

YOUTH #1. The blighter took forever to die, didn't he?

YOUTH #3. More fight from our former friend than we expected. What we need is wine.

YOUTH #1. A blighting toast then, to us and to the gold.

YOUTHS #1 & #3. To the gold! (*THEY drink, and then die horrible, highly theatrical deaths. When they're finally dead, the UNDERTAKER enters.*)

UNDERTAKER. (*Fondling the gold.*) Well, didn't I warn them? Death isn't hard to find. He can often be found walking hand in hand with greed. (*Long horrifying laugh as he exits.*)

ALL YOUTHS. (*As they clear the stage.*)
Did you ever think when a hearse goes by,
That you might be the next to die?
You toss and turn until you're green,
Then puss comes out like fresh whipped cream.

STORYTELLERS.
Make no mistake.
There are people who give
And people who take.

STORYTELLER. A native American story!
STORYTELLERS. NANABOZO AND THE BOULDER!
(*Ad lib comments by the performers will help the audience join into the spirit of the story as traditionally the listeners make rude comments on Nanabozo's behavior.*)

NARRATOR. Nanabozo was walking along the road. It was a beautiful day and Nanabozo was as happy as happy could be. He was wearing his most beautiful headdress. He had painted his face with great style and many additional flourishes. Most importantly, he carried his wonderful blanket which was large and colorful and a perfect complement to his outfit.

NANABOZO. How many friends and relatives in the next village will admire me . . .

NARRATOR. Thought Nanabozo.

NANABOZO. And how all the girls will faint with pleasure when they see me pass.

NARRATOR. And he went on . . .

NANABOZO. Surely I am the most handsome of men.

NARRATOR. The birds and animals stopped and stared as he passed by.

GIVE AND TAKE 17

NANABOZO. How they wish the could be as splendid as I . . .

NARRATOR. Thought Nanabozo.

ANIMALS & BIRDS. What a conceited jerk . . .

NARRATOR. Thought the animals and birds. And they laughed. And laughed. And laughed. But still Nanabozo strutted on. Before too long the sun began to rise high in the sky.

SUN. Up and up I go.

NARRATOR. And Nanabozo, burdened by all of his best clothes began to get very warm.

NANABOZO. Ah, Sun, please be kind.

SUN. Yeah, right.

NARRATOR. Said the Sun. The sweat poured from Nanabozo's body, and his face paint begain to melt.

NANABOZO. It is too hot to go forward. I will rest in the shade of that boulder.

NARRATOR. Said Nanabozo as he collapsed.

NANABOZO. Oh, why did I bring my blanket? It is smothering me . . .

NARRATOR. Whined Nanabozo as he reclined in the shade of the boulder. Then suddenly, an idea occured to him and he jumped to his feet.

NANABOZO. Poor, poor Grandfather Boulder . . .

NARRATOR. Said Nanabozo.

NANABOZO. Even while you give me shade, you are trapped in the sun, unable to protect yourself from its ruthlessness.

SUN. Yeah, right . . .

NARRATOR. Said the Sun. Ignoring him, Nanabozo went on.

NANABOZO. I can be as generous as you, Grandfather.

Here, I will drape my blanket to protect you from the Sun . . .

NARRATOR. Said Nanabozo as he did just that. Then he merrily went on his way, no longer burdened by the blanket. (*NANABOZO starts whistling.*) But before long, dark thunder clouds emerged from over the mountains . . .

CLOUDS. Rumble, rumble, rumble.

NARRATOR. And covered the Sun.

SUN. Hi, Clouds.

CLOUDS. Hi, Sun.

NARRATOR. Nanabozo grew afraid.

NANABOZO. If it rains, my beautiful clothes will be ruined . . .

NARRATOR. Said Nanabozo as he hurried back to retrieve his blanket.

NANABOZO. I guess you won't need this anymore, Boulder, since the Sun no longer shines.

NARRATOR. And he grabbed his blanket and ran. Soon it started to rain . . .

RAIN. Pitter patter, pitter patter.

NARRATOR. And thunder . . .

CLOUDS. Rumble, rumble, rumble.

NARRATOR. And lightning.

LIGHTNING. Crack, crack, zizzle.

NARRATOR. And Nanabozo sheltered himself in his blanket to protect his clothes.

NANABOZO. Dry and safe . . .

NARRATOR. He thought. But underneath the sound of the storm, he heard another, more foreboding sound.

BOULDER. Bump, Bump, Bump.

NARRATOR. He peeked out from beneath his blanket to see what it could be.

BOULDER. Bump, Bump, Bump.

GIVE AND TAKE 19

NARRATOR. And there, to his horror, he saw . . .
BOULDER. The Boulder.
NANABOZO. The Boulder?
NARRATOR. The Boulder. And it was smashing across the plains straight at him.
BOULDER. Bump.
NANABOZO. Ahhhhh!
NARRATOR. Screamed Nanabozo, and throwing aside his blanket he fled.
NARRATOR. He ran this way. He ran that way. But still the Boulder followed.
NANABOZO. Ahhhh!
BOULDER. Bump, bump, bump.
NANABOZO. I'll climb to the top of the mountain; a boulder can't roll up a mountain . . .
NARRATOR. Thought Nanabozo. But the Boulder came right up after him.
NANABOZO. Ahhhh!
BOULDER. Bump, bump, bump.
NARRATOR. Finally, Nanabozo thought . . .
NANABOZO. I'll swim across the river. If the Boulder tries to follow, he'll sink right to the bottom.
NARRATOR. So, he swam across the river, and collapsed in an exhausted heap on the other side.
NANABOZO. Pant, pant, pant.
NARRATOR. But the Boulder . . .
BOULDER Bump, bump, bump.
NARRATOR. With a surge of power, leaped across the river, and landed right on Nanabozo's feet.
NANABOZO. Ahhhh!
NARRABOZO. Screamed Nanabozo.
BOULDER. Bump.

NARRATOR. Sighed the Boulder. At that moment, the clouds parted.

CLOUDS. Bye, Sun.

SUN. Bye, Clouds.

NARRATOR. And once again, it grew very hot. Roasting and in pain, Nanabozo pleaded with the Boulder.

NANABOZO. Good, kind, Boulder, let me go, I beg of you. I will give you my headdress, my fine clothes, my blanket – anything. Just get off my feet.

NARRATOR. But the Boulder replied with an obviously negative . . .

BOULDER. Bump.

NARRATOR. Then, noticing the animals and birds that he passed earlier in the day, Nanabozo said . . .

NANABOZO. Brothers, I beg you, give me your help. This evil Boulder is trying to kill me.

NARRATOR. But the animals replied . . .

ANIMALS & BIRDS. Why should we give you anything? All you know how to do is take. So take your punishment. You got just what you deserved.

NARRATOR. And they laughed as they wandered off.

ANIMALS & BIRDS. Ha, ha, ha. Let's get out of this steaming hot Sun.

NANABOZO. Ahhh!

ANIMALS & BIRDS. Let's go get a nice cool drink.

NANABOZO. Ahhh!

NARRATOR. And Nanabozo was left alone with the Boulder. Eventually, night fell.

SUN. Down and down and down I go.

NARRATOR. And the Moon rose.

MOON. Up and up and up I go.

NARRATOR. And the bats came out.

BATS. Squeek, squeek, squeek.
NARRATOR. And Nanabozo thought of a plan.
NANABOZO. Hey, Bats.
BATS. Squeek?
NANABOZO. Boulder here says you are ugly.
BATS. Squeek?
NANABOZO. He says you are so ugly, that you're embarrassed to come out in the daytime.
BATS. Squeek?
NANABOZO. He said that you are the most disgustingly ugly creatures in creation!
BATS. He did? He said that?
NANABOZO. And worse, but I couldn't possibly repeat what else he said about you.
BATS. Let's get him, guys! Bats, attack. (*THEY dive-bomb Boulder, making the appropriate noises.*)
NARRATOR. And they did just that. Making assault after assault on the Boulder. Chipping away at him until pieces of the rock were thrown all across the plains. Finally, the Boulder was completely disintegrated. And Nanabozo moved his damaged feet.
NANABOZO. Well, I guess you showed him a lesson.
NARRATOR. But the Bat's only response was laughter.
BATS. Ha, ha, ha.
NANABOZO. What's so funny?
NARRATOR. Asked Nanabozo.
BATS. You!
NANABOZO. Me?
BATS. If the Boulder thought us ugly, imagine what he thought of you . . .
NARRATOR. Laughed the Bats.
NANABOZO. What are you talking about? Am I not the

most handsome, well-dressed man on the plains?

NARRATOR. At this the Bats burst into uproarious gales of laughter.

BATS. Handsome! Look at you, you're covered with mud, your hair is matted and your face paint is smeared. Well-dressed! Why you are almost naked except for a few tatters of clothing! You don't even have a blanket to cover you!

NARRATOR. And the Bats flew laughing into the night.

NANABOZO. It's true . . .

NARRATOR. Thought Nanabozo as he looked himself over.

NANABOZO. Poor me. I am the most homely and poorly-dressed of men without even a blanket to cover me.

NARRATOR. And sighing hugely . . .

NANABOZO. Sigh!

NARRATOR. And beginning to weep in self-pity . . .

NANABOZO. Weep, weep, weep.

NARRATOR. Nanabozo began to walk along the road towards the village.

STORYTELLERS.
Make no mistake.
There are people who give
And people who take.

STORYTELLER. A Japanese legend!
STORYTELLERS. THE CRANE WIFE!

(One set of actors will portray the characters by wearing masks and engaging in slow stylized movement. Another set of actors will provide the voices for the characters.)

NARRATOR. High atop a mountain in Japan, where the

winter mind and cold can steal the breath from your body, lived a poor man named Yohei. One morning in early winter, Yohei fled from the chill of his small hut into the neighboring fields in order to scavenge some wood to warm his dwelling. As he was climbing around a large rock, he saw a crane piteously plucking at an arrow which some hunter had shot into its wing. Yohei calmed the bird, removed the arrow and tenderly repaired the damage to the bird's extremity. After seeing the bird safely into the sky, Yohei searched for wood, but finding none, returned with dread to his icy abode. The day passed into night. The cold grew deeper, more intense and seemed to reach into Yohei's very soul, bringing with it hopelessness and despair.

YOHEI. Oh, to be warm.

NARRATOR. Cried Yohei.

YOHEI. Will I ever be warm again?

NARRATOR. At that moment, there was a knock at the door, and answering it, Yohei found a beautiful young woman.

CRANE WIFE. I have come. You have cried for warmth, and I have come.

YOHEI. I don't understand. Who are you? Why have you come to me?

CRANE WIFE. I have come because you have called. I am to be your wife, if you will have me.

NARRATOR. Astounded at his good fortune, Yohei agreed without hesitation to marry the beautiful stranger. Soon his life was happier than he ever thought possible. His wife filled their home with love and warmth, and for a while Yohei ceased to be cold. But some things had not changed. He was still poor, and found it almost impossible to feed an extra mouth. He worried and grew anxious.

CRANE WIFE. Husband, what is it that brings you pain?

Will you not tell me so that I may share the burden?

YOHEI. The winter is long, and our food supply is short. There is no money to buy more. It grows cold. Daily it grows more cold, can you not feel it?

NARRATOR. After thinking carefully, his wife responded . . .

CRANE WIFE. Other wives help their husbands by weaving cloth that can be sold for money. If it is your desire, I will do this also.

YOHEI. You will do this for me?

CRANE WIFE. I will do this thing, but one promise you must make me: you must not watch while I weave the cloth.

YOHEI. I will so promise.

NARRATOR. Then the dutiful wife went into the back room of the hut, and the sound of her weaving issued forth. For three days and three nights she weaved, and on the morning of the fourth day she left the room and presented a bolt of beautiful white silken fabric to her husband.

YOHEI. Why, it is beyond beautiful . . .

NARRATOR. Said the grateful husband. Then turning to his wife, he noticed that she had grown quite pale and weak with her efforts.

YOHEI. Beloved wife, are you ill from your weaving?

CRANE WIFE. The cost of the weaving is great, but worth it to see you warmed by what I have created. Go husband, sell the fabric, and buy what supplies we need for this winter.

NARRATOR. And Yohei did just that, bringing the beautiful cloth to the village where it was much admired, and where it brought a good price.

YOHEI. How fortunate am I to have such a wife . . .

NARRATOR. He thought. But the winter continued, and

after many weeks, their supplies dwindled, and once again Yohei grew worried, and once again the chill of despair enclosed his heart.

CRANE WIFE. Husband, what is it that brings you such pain? Will you not tell me that I may share the burden?

YOHEI. The winter is long, and once again our food supply grows short. There is no money to buy more. It grows cold. Daily it grows more cold, can you not feel it?

CRANE WIFE. You wish me to weave again?

YOHEI. You will do this thing for me?

CRANE WIFE. I will do this thing, but I beg you, let it be the last time.

YOHEI. I promise.

CRANE WIFE. And you must not watch while I weave the cloth.

YOHEI. This too I promise.

NARRATOR. So once again the dutiful wife went into the back room of the hut, and once again she weaved, and on the morning of the fifth day she left the room and presented a bolt of beautiful white silken fabric to her husband.

YOHEI. Why, this is even more beautiful than the last . . .

NARRATOR. Said the grateful husband. Then turning to his wife, he noticed that she had grown even more pale and weak than the last time. Indeed, she could barely remain standing.

YOHEI. Beloved wife, are you ill from your weaving?

CRANE WIFE. The cost of weaving is great, but worth it to see you warmed by what I have created. Go husband, sell the fabric, and buy what supplies we need for the winter.

NARRATOR. And Yohei did just that, bringing the beautiful cloth to the village where it was much admired, and where it brought an even greater price than before.

YOHEI. How fortunate I am to have such a wife . . .

NARRATOR. He thought. But as he was returning home, he was met on the road by his Neighbor who stopped him.

NEIGHBOR. Yohei, my good friend, how fortunate you are to have a wife who weaves so beautifully.

YOHEI. Thank you, good neighbor.

NEIGHBOR. It's too bad you have wasted such beautiful fabric by selling it to the fools in the village.

YOHEI. Why should I not sell it to them; they paid a fair price for it.

NEIGHBOR. A fair price from the village is not a fair price from the city.

YOHEI. The city?

NEIGHBOR. Yes, tell your wife to weave more fabric and I will bring it to the city to sell for you. It will bring a fortune and you will be rich beyond your dreams.

YOHEI. But the cost to my wife of such weaving is great.

NEIGHBOR. If she truly loves you . . .

NARRATOR. Said the Neighbor . . .

NEIGHBOR. No cost would be too dear. If she truly loves you, she will do what she must to make you happy.

NARRATOR. And saying so, the Neighbor left him. Yohei returned home and tried to act happy, but he was tormented by the thought of all the riches he might possess if only his wife could . . .

CRANE WIFE. Husband, what is it that brings you such pain? Have not our burdens been lifted? We have supplies enough to last through the longest winter, and you led me to believe that you are pleased with me.

YOHEI. I am pleased, I am pleased, but . . .

CRANE WIFE. Speak husband, that I may share this burden.

YOHEI. Oh my wife, the world is a cold, cold place and I am daily made colder by the thought of riches within my grasp if only . . .

CRANE WIFE. You wish me to weave again.

YOHEI. You will do this thing for me?

CRANE WIFE. I will do this thing, but it brings me great sorrow to hear you ask.

YOHEI. Oh, wife, I promise I will never ask again.

CRANE WIFE. And you must promise not to watch me while I weave.

YOHEI. I do so promise.

NARRATOR. And for the last time, the dutiful wife went into the back room of the hut, and the sound of her weaving issued forth. For five days and five nights she weaved, and on the morning of the sixth day, she did not leave the room, but continued to weave throughout the day and into the night. Yohei grew anxious.

YOHEI. What can be taking so long?

NARRATOR. And through that night and into the next day she continued to weave. Yohei grew cold with fear, and called . . .

YOHEI. Are you all right? Can you hear me?

NARRATOR. But the only response was the sound of the loom. Finally, the husband could wait no longer, and burst into the back room of the hut.

CRANE WIFE. Ahhhhhh!

NARRATOR. The sight before him froze him to the spot. For at the loom was a crane, covered in blood from where it had plucked its own feathers to feed into the loom. And the Crane spoke to him . . .

CRANE WIFE. I am the crane whose wing you mended. I fell in love with your gentleness and returned in human form to spend my life with you. But now, despite your promise, you have looked upon my suffering, and I must leave.

NARRATOR. And the beautiful bird extended its wings and sailed into the sky, flying towards the horizon.

YOHEI. Come back . . .

NARRATOR. Yohei cried.

YOHEI. Come back and I will cherish you.

NARRATOR. But the bird was gone. And on the floor beneath the loom, was a bolt of fabric so beautiful that it appeared magical. And the cloth was pure white with streaks of red from the blood of the crane.

YOHEI. Oh my wife!

NARRATOR. And though Yohei wrapped the beautiful cloth around him again and again, he could not get warm. And he was never warm again.

STORYTELLERS.

Make no mistake.
There are people who give
And people who take.

A STORYTELLER. From the steppes of Russia . . .

STORYTELLERS. STRIDING SLIPPERS! (*Each time someone dons the slippers, Russian music should begin, followed by energetic Russian dancing.*)

SHEPHERD. Once upon a time there was a shepherd who had many cows and sheep to take care of. Now, cows and sheep are not the most intelligent of animals, and the poor shepherd would wear himself out trying to keep them all together and out of trouble. At the end of each day his bones would ache, his head would pound, and his poor feet would scream in pain. Then one day, when he could take no more, he came up with a plan. "I know," said the Shepherd, "I will

will make me a pair of slippers out of the bark of the linden tree, and cushion them with wool from the sheep." And he did just that. When he was finished, he discovered that the slippers were not only comfortable, but they allowed him to move across the fields swiftly and with great ease. "Ah, me! Such joy I have from my striding slippers!" said the Shepherd, as he sat in the shade of a tree. (*He takes off the slippers to better admire them.*)

STRANGER. Just then, a Stranger happened along the road, and, greeting the Shepherd, sat beside him to share the shade. "It's a very large herd, you have," said the Stranger, "How does one person take care of so many animals?"

SHEPHERD. "Oh, it used to be a terrible problem," said the Shepherd, "but since I made these striding slippers, my life is perfect. Every step I take carries me across the field."

STRANGER. "My, aren't you lucky," said the Stranger. But to himself he thought, "My slippers are worn to tatters, and I still have many miles to go before I reach my cousin's house. His slippers are not only new, but he claims they have almost magical properties. I want those slippers!"

SHEPHERD. "Did you say something?"

STRANGER. "Good heavens, is that a wolf lurking near your sheep?"

SHEPHERD. "Where? Where?" asked the trusting Shepherd, forgetting all about his slippers.

STRANGER. "Over there," said the Stranger, pointing away. And as the Shepherd turned to search for the wolf, the Stranger grabbed his slippers and put them on his feet. And before he knew it, the slippers carried him off like the wind.

SHEPHERD. "Hey! Come back, come back with my slippers!"

STRANGER. But even if he wanted to, the Stranger had

no idea of how to control the slippers.

SHEPHERD. And, of course, there was no way that the Shepherd could catch him.

STRANGER. Across the fields and down the road the slippers carried him. "Wait! Stop! That's my cousin's village!!!" But still the slippers kept going. The Stranger threw himself to the ground to try to stop, but still the slippers kept his feet in motion.

CHILDREN. All the children in the village gathered around him, and laughed to see such a silly sight.

STRANGER. "Help! Take the slippers off of my feet and I will give you candy!" said the Stranger.

CHILDREN. And the Children, after much effort, managed to do just that.

STRANGER. "Seven times seven curses on those striding slippers," screamed the still-frightened Stranger. "I'm lucky you got them off, or I might have spent the rest of my life running down the roads of the world," he said to the Children as he distributed candy. When he was done, he carried the slippers into the house where he was greeted warmly by his cousin.

COUSIN. "Cousin, how good to see you! But why do you come barefoot?" asked the bemused relative.

STRANGER. The Stranger was ashamed that he had stolen the slippers, so he lied. "Ah, these blasted slippers are too small for me and pinch my feet."

COUSIN. "Let me try them," said the Cousin, "Maybe they'll fit me and we can trade."

STRANGER. The Stranger protested, but before he knew it, his cousin had put the slippers on his feet.

COUSIN. "Why, these are perrrrrrfffffect," said the Cousin as the slippers began to move. "What the . . .

Help!!!"

STRANGER. But before help arrived, the slippers carried the Cousin out the door and into the road.

COUSIN. "Heeeeeeellllllpppppp!" the Cousin continued to cry, but the slippers led him into the forest where finally he was knocked unconscious by a low-hanging limb. "Argh!"

MERCHANT. At this moment a greedy Merchant happened by and saw the poor Cousin. "You, are you alive?"

COUSIN. "Barely."

MERCHANT. "Are you drunk?"

COUSIN. "Of course not. It's these blasted slippers. Seven times seventy curses on them. The minute I put them on, they carried me a mile down the road in the blink of an eye. Too fast for me. I could have killed myself on that tree."

MERCHANT. The Merchant immediately grew interested. "Hmmm," he thought, "if these slippers are really that fast, think of the work I could get out of my servant who is so slow and lazy." He approached the Cousin. "Well, my good man, it's obvious that those slippers are quite dangerous. Why don't you give them to me?"

COUSIN. "Why should I do that?"

MERCHANT. "Because I will give you two kopecs for them. With two kopecs y;ou can buy a nice safe pair of slippers.

COUSIN. "It's a deal," said the Cousin, exchanging the slippers for the kopecs. Then he walked back to the village, glad to have survived his adventure.

MERCHANT. The Merchant also hurried home, anxious to try the slippers on his servant. "You, slowpoke, get over here. I want you to clean out the barn, gather firewood, harvest the cabbages and water the animals. Do you understand?"

SERVANT. "Yup," said the Servant.

MERCHANT. "But first put these slippers on; they will help you to get your work done faster."

SERVANT. "Okay," said the Servant, putting on the slippers. "OOOOOOHHHHH . . . . "

MERCHANT. But almost before he could stand, the bumbling Servant was carried like a whirlwind to the barn, where he terrified the animals, who broke loose and fled. "You stupid fool, go after them."

SERVANT. "I'm a-trying, but these slippers have a mind of their own," said the Servant as he threw himself to the ground."

MERCHANT. "Nincompoop!" screamed the Merchant. "Give them to me, I'll show you how it's done." And so saying, he tore the slippers from the Servant's feet and put them on his own. In a flash, he was off.

SERVANT. But instead of chasing the animals, the slippers took him in the opposite direction and crashed the Merchant into the barn, then into a fence, then into several trees. The Merchant did not look happy.

MERCHANT. "AHHHHH! Help, you fool! Take these blasted slippers off my feet!"

SERVANT. But the poor old Servant was too slow to catch the Merchant. "Bye-bye."

MERCHANT. Then he flew out the gate, through several puddles, across a couple of particularly rough fields, into a river, and through the woods where he tripped over a tree stump;. "Ouchh! Help, save me! Somebody get these blasted slippers off my feet!!! They are killing me!"

SHEPHERD. And who should hear his cries, but the Shepherd, who followed the sound of his voice. "Hey, those are my slippers!" said the Shepherd as he yanked them off the

Merchant's feet.

MERCHANT. "Seven times seven hundred curses," he screamed. But seeing a possible profit in the transaction, the greedy Merchant said, "I might be willing to sell these wonderful slippers to you."

SHEPHERD. "Sell me my own slippers!" cried the Shepherd. "Why, you must be the thief who stole them!" And he went after the Merchant with his staff.

MERCHANT. It was amazing how fast the Merchant could move even without the striding slippers.

SHEPHERD. And the Shepherd allowed him to escape, because he was a peace-loving man. When the Merchant had quite disappeared, the Shepherd put the slippers on his feet. "Ah, seven times seven thousand blessings!"

STRANGER. And the happy Shepherd returned to his flock.

COUSIN. Everyone said that he was the best Shepherd in the land.

SERVANT. He never lost a single cow or calf or sheep . . .

MERCHANT. No matter how far they strayed.

SHEPHERD. And never in his life did he feel tired again.

STORYTELLERS.

Yes, there are people who give

And people who take. (*Repeat as actors leave the stage.*)

* * *

ACT TWO

(STORYTELLERS burst on to the stage accompanied by blasts of music)

STORYTELLERS. Giiiiiiiiiiiiiiiiiivvvveee and . . .

LEPRECHAUN. BRIDGET AND THE LEPRECHAUN – a bit of Irish whimsy!

BRIDGET. One morning Bridget set out as usual to draw a bucket of water from the well near her house, but, when she got there, she found the well dry. So, in disgust she trudged across the fields to use the well by the old abandoned monastery. As she grumbled along she heard a sound.

LEPRECHAUN. Tap, tap tap.

BRIDGET. She immediately wondered if it could possibly be . . .

LEPRECHAUN. A Leprechaun. Everyone knows that the magical little cobblers had to come up from underground to do their job – which was the mending of the shoes for the Little People.

BRIDGET. Suddenly Bridget's mood lightened, because if you could catch a leprechaun, and keep him in your sight, he'd have to give you his pot of gold.

LEPRECHAUN. Call it what it is: robbery plain and simple.

BRIDGET. "Merciful heavens", thought Bridget, "this is me chance to be a rich woman!" So she put her bucket aside, and crept along the hedge 'til she caught sight of him.

LEPRECHAUN. And what a good looking little man he was, sitting there happily tapping away without a care in the world, until suddenly . . .

BRIDGET. Bridget sprang from behind the hedge, grabbed him by the throat and said, "I'll be having that pot of gold if you don't mind."

LEPRECHAUN. "Help. Help! I'm being assaulted. Help! Help! Murder!"

BRIDGET. "Now stop it with your carrying on. It's just a young girl, I am."

LEPRECHAUN. "A young girl you may be, but you can still choke the very life out of a man. Let me go!"

BRIDGET. "I'll be doing that, as soon as you're after giving me your pot of gold."

LEPRECHAUN. "Sure now, a beautiful young thing like yourself wouldn't hurt a body."

BRIDGET. "I'll be cutting off your head if the gold isn't soon forthcoming."

LEPRECHAUN. "But I'm just a poor cobbler."

BRIDGET. "All right then, if that's what you want, we'll be going."

LEPRECHAUN. "Where would you be taking me?"

BRIDGET. "To the village. If you won't be telling me where the gold is, I'll be giving you to me brother, Seamus, who's after being a blacksmith. The strongest arms in the county, they say, and he'll be quick about squeezin' the truth out of you."

LEPRECHAUN. "Wait. Stop. It's giving in, I know when I'm bested."

BRIDGET. "All right, then. It's the truth I'll be having."

LEPRCHAUN. "And it's the truth I'll give you. Though who would have thought such a delicate, beautiful young . . ."

BRIDGET. "Enough of that blather. You'll be taking me to the gold. Now."

LEPRECHAUN. "All right. Let me go, and I'll be leading you there."

BRIDGET. "You must be thinking I was born yesterday. I'll not be letting the likes of you go 'til the treasure's in me hand."

LEPRECHAUN. "But it's terrible far away and I'll make no time at all with your hand around me throat."

BRIDGET. "Then I'll be holding you by the britches."

LEPRECHAUN. "Stop, let me go!" cried the Leprechaun. "I'll be after being the laughing stock of the Little People with you holding onto me trousers."

BRIDGET. "You'll be getting a move on, or it'll be into the well with you, me little man."

LEPRECHAUN. And so he led her . . .

BRIDGET. Under the hedge . . .

LEPRECHAUN. Over a wall . . .

BRIDGET. Across the field. But still Bridget held on to him.

LEPRECHAUN. And then he led her . . .

BRIDGET. Through a creek . . .

LEPRECHAUN. Over a hill . . .

BRIDGET. Around a growth of trees. But still he could not tire her.

LEPRECHAUN. "It's inhuman you are. Aren't you ever after getting me weary, my girl?"

BRIDGET. "That pot of gold will be keeping me going for as long as it takes."

LEPRECHAUN. "All right, then. I'm giving it up. The gold is over there."

BRIDGET. And the Little Man led her out into a field of tall yellow flowers.

LEPRECHAUN. "There it is, under that flower. Dig there and you'll get your gold."

BRIDGET. "Dig?"

LEPRECHAUN. "You'll have to be digging a great hole, maybe ten feet or more."

BRIDGET. "And how will I be doing that, my fine man?"

LEPRECHAUN. "Why with a shovel, how else? You best go and get one before darkness falls."

BRIDGET. "All right. Let's be hurrying then."

LEPRECHAUN. "I'll not be going with, not I. I haven't the strength to take another step. And besides, someone will have to stay here to protect it from the other Little People. They're after being terrible thieves and liars, you know."

BRIDGET. "And how do I know that you'll be sitting here when I get back?"

LEPRECHAUN. "So young, you are, and already so suspicious. I'll make a bit of a deal with you. I'll tie this ribbon around the flower, so even if something should be happening to me – like getting kidnapped for the second time today – you'll still know where to be looking."

BRIDGET. "And what if you have a mind to take the ribbon off as soon as I'm gone?"

LEPRECHAUN. "It's a terrible untrusting nature you have, isn't it? All right, then, I'll give you the most solemn Leprechaun oath to soothe your doubting mind. If I remove the ribbon from this flower, may all the gold I own and ever will own, turn to dust in me hands. There now, are ye satisfied?"

BRIDGET. And, indeed, Bridget was. She flew past the flowers as if the devil himself were after her. Around the trees, down the hill, through the creek, across the field, over the wall, under the hedge, past the well and into the barn by her house where she grabbed a shovel. Then without pausing for breath, away she ran past the well, under the hedge, over the wall, across the field, through the creek, up the hill, around the trees and into the mass of yellow flowers.

LEPRECHAUN. The first thing she realized when she got

back to the field, was that the Leprechaun had disappeared without a trace.

BRIDGET. "Thank heavens I made him swear not to touch the ribbon on the flower," said Bridget, still gasping for breath.

LEPRECHAUN. The second thing she realized was a bit more shocking. For when she looked around her at the field of yellow flowers, she saw that every single one of them had a ribbon attached to it.

BRIDGET. "No", screamed Bridget. "No, no!" And set to shovelling like a mad woman.

LEPRECHAUN. But she never did find the gold.

BRIDGET. And she never left her house without a shovel again.

STORYTELLERS.
Make no mistake.
There are people who give
And people who take.

A STORYTELLER. From Nigeria . . .

STORYTELLERS. KALULU AND THE MONEY FARM! (*Animal masks or pieces of masks might help suggest both the characters and the culture.*)

NARRATOR One planting time, just before the seasonal rains started, the Chief ordered each of the animals to plant certain crops.

CHIEF. Warthog, I want you to grow yams.

WARTHOG. Yo.

CHIEF. Lion, you take care of the sorghum.

LION. Cool, dude.

CHIEF. Tortoise, from you I want corn. Lots and lots of corn.

GIVE AND TAKE

TORTOISE. Duh, okay, chief.

CHIEF. And you rabbit . . .

KALULU. That's Hare. I'm a hare and my name's Kalulu.

CHIEF. Is that respect? Is that how you talk with respect to your chief? I get very angry when I feel disrespected.

KALULU. Sorry, Chief. But I got this great idea . . .

CHIEF. I will decide what idea is great. Tell me.

KALULU. Chief, if you give me a bag of money to use as seed, I will grow such a large crop of money from it, that you will be rich!

CHIEF. Who are you trying to fool? Money don't grow on no trees.

KALULU. I know the secret.

CHIEF. The secret?

KALULU. The secret that will make you rich, rich, rich!

CHIEF. Rich, rich, rich?

KALULU. Take a chance, Chief. This is an offer you can't refuse. Easy money!

NARRATOR. The Chief, attracted by the idea of easy money, decided to trust Kalulu.

CHIEF. Here is a bag of money. Tend your garden carefully and bring me the money when it is harvested. Don't disappoint me. Disappointment makes me mad.

KALULU. Don't worry, Chief. You're going to be rich, rich, rich.

NARRATOR. But of cousre, Kalulu had no intention of planting the money. Instead, he bought fine clothes to wear, expensive delicacies to eat, and new jewelry for his wife.

KALULU. Ah, this is the life.

KALULU'S WIFE. But what are you going to do when the harvest is in?

KALULU. I'll think of something. Don't worry; be happy.

NARRATOR. But soon it was the harvest time and the Chief sent for Kalulu.

CHIEF. Where is the money you promised to grow?

KALULU. Chief, Chief, Chief, don't you know anything? Money is a very slow-growing crop. Perhaps it will be ready next year.

NARRATOR. But the next year came, and then the year after that, and still Kalulu had no money for the Chief. The Chief grew impatient.

CHIEF. You are disappointing me.

KALULU. But . . .

CHIEF. Warthog, you are the most trustworthy of my animals. Go with Kalulu to his money farm and bring me the harvest.

WARTHOG. Yo, boss. Let's go.

NARRATOR. Kalulu turned white with fear. As they walked along he said . . .

KALULU. Ah., Warthog, I can't go on. I'm sick, dying . . . and the walk is too far.

WARTHOG. Not for nothing, but I could care less. I have my orders. Keep walking.

KALULU. Oh, no, I just remembered. We'll have to sleep at the farm tonight, and I forgot my pillow. I'll be right back.

WARTHOG. But . . .

KALULU. Keep going, I'll catch up.

NARRATOR. But secretly, Kalulu sneaked around in front of the Warthog, and disguising his voice he screamed . . .

KALULU. I see a fat Warthog! Come along fellow hunters, supper's there waiting to be killed. (*Running around to make it seem like many people*) Over here, over there, this way.

WARTHOG. No way I'm gonna be someone's main course.

NARRATOR. And Warthog ran home as fast as his stubby little legs could take him.

WARTHOG. Maaaaaammmmmmmaaa!

NARRATOR. Then Kalulu went back to the Chief and said . . .

KALULU. Gee, Chief, I can't imagine what happened. Something must have scared Warthog 'cause he took off like a bat out of you know where.

CHIEF. Warthogs can be very moody. Lion, you are the bravest of my animals. Go with Kahlulu to his money farm and bring back the harvest.

LION. No prob, dude.

NARRATOR. Kalulu started shaking with fear. Now he wa really in trouble. How was he supposed to scare the Lion, bravest of all creatures?

KALULU. Ah, Lion, I forgot my hoe. I'll run home and get it. Won't take me a minute.

LION That's cool, little dude. I'll just lie here and chill til you get back.

KALULU. Okay, but be careful. They say there are evil spirits in this forest.

LION. Like, dude, you're playing with my head. Be cool. You know there's no such things as spirits.

KALULU. Well . . .

LION. Book it, dude. I'm cool.

NARRATOR. And the Lion settled into an uneasy sleep. (*As the Lion falls asleep, Kalulu sneaks up to him and screams spirit noises*)

KALULU. AAAARRRRRRGGGGGHHHH!

LION. Aaaahhhhhh!!!

NARRATOR. And the lion was so startled that he ran like the wind.

LION. This is so uncool. I'm like out of here.

NARRATOR. Once again, Kalulu went back to the Chief and told him the news.

CHIEF. Lions can be very high strung.

KALULU. It certainly looks that way.

CHIEF. Tortoise, you are the most sensible of all my animals. Go with Kalulu to the money farm and bring back the harvest.

TORTOISE. Duh, okay.

NARRATOR. This time Kalulu was more relaxed. After all, a clever fellow like him could certainly out think a slow-witted creature like the Tortoise.

KALULU. Ah, Tortoise, I better go back. I've forgotten my pillow.

TORTOISE. That's okay. You can borrow mine.

NARRATOR. Said the Tortoise, removing a pillow from his shell.

KALULU. Oh. Ah, Tortoise, I definitely have to go back, now. I forgot my hoe.

TORTOISE. That's okay, I brought an extra, just in case.

NARRATOR. Said the Tortoise, removing a hoe from his shell.

KALULU. You know, Tortoise, terrible spirits live in this forest. That's what scared Lion. Can't you hear them? (*He attempts to throw his voice*) I better run home and get my charms.

TORTOISE. You're a funny guy, Kalulu. But you can't trick me, I saw your lips move.

KALULU. No, really you must be mistaken. There are spirits and . . . Ahhhh! (*Starts screaming and thrashing as if possessed*) Help, help, leave me alone! (*Runs off yelling*)

TORTOISE. Hey, get back here. You're gonna get in trouble. The Chief ain't gonna be happy about this.

NARRATOR. Kalulu, knowing that the Tortoise saw through his trick, ran back to his hut to seek his wife's help.

KALULU. Wife, wife! Help me. Hide me. They know I cheated the Chief.

KALULU'S WIFE. You cheated the chief?

KALULU. I cheated the Chief.

KALULU'S WIFE. It will be death for you.

KALULU. Hide me!

KALULU'S WIFE. There's no place to hide.

KALULU. I have it! Pull out all my hair and pretend I'm your baby.

KALULU'S WIFE. That's crazy.

KALULU. It's the only way to save me!

KALULU'S WIFE. All right, but this is going to hurt. (*She pulls out his hair as he screams*)

NARRATOR. It wasn't long before the Chief himself arrived at the hut.

CHIEF. Where is Kalulu?

KALULU'S WIFE. I don't know. As you can see the only people here are me and my baby.

CHIEF. You're hiding him.

KALULU'S WIFE. Where is there to hide?

CHIEF. You must know where he is.

KALULU'S WIFE. I tell you, I don't.

CHIEF. Well then, give me the child. I'll hold him hostage until Kalulu delivers my money.

KALULU'S WIFE. No!

CHIEF. Yes! Give him to me!

KALULU'S WIFE. Won't you at least allow me to say goodbye to my child?

CHIEF. Well then, hurry up.

KALULU'S WIFE. My poor baby . . . (*whispering*) In the morning, when I bring breakfast, pretend you are dead.

KALULU. What?

CHIEF. What was that?

KALULU'S WIFE. Just the baby crying.

KALULU. Whaaaaa!

KALULU'S WIFE. If I may, I will bring him food in the morning.

CHIEF. All right, all right.

NARRATOR. And the Chief left with his little hostage. The next morning, when Kalulu's Wife opened the blanket, she cried . . .

KALULU'S WIFE. My baby! My baby is dead! (*to the Chief*) You killed my baby. Murderer!

CHIEF. Well, I didn't mean any disrespect. It must have been an accident.

NARRATOR. But before long, the Chief was as upset as Kalulu's Wife, and started crying with her.

CHIEF. I'm sorry. So sorry. What can I do to ease your grief?

KALULU (*Throwing his voice*) Money.

CHIEF. Did you hear something?

KALULU. Money, you buffoon.

CHIEF. Here, will this help? (*Handing her a bag of money*)

KALULU'S WIFE. Nothing can bring back my child.

CHIEF. No disrespect intended.

KALULU'S WIFE. But a woman must eat. (*Taking the money and leaving*)

NARRATOR. A month or so later, when his hair grew back, Kalulu returned to the Chief.

KALULU. Well, Chief, I'm afraid it wasn't much of a crop. (*Hands him the money*)

CHIEF. All that work, and there's no more money now than what you started with.

KALULU. It just goes to show you, Chief.

CHIEF. What?

KALULU. There's no such thing as easy money.

STORYTELLERS.
Make no mistake.
There are people who give
And people who take.

STORYTELLER. An Italian tale!

STORYTELLERS. THE MOST PRECIOUS POSSESSION!

ANSALDO. In the days before Columbus bumped into the North American continent on his way to China, there were many other great Italian sailors and navigators searching out new trade routes. Some, like Ansaldo, were as interested in the adventure of exploration as they were in the riches to be had from commercial success.

GIOCONDO. There were others, however, like Giocondo the Magnificent, who lusted after profit like a desert lusts for rain.

ANSALDO. It so happened that these two men, both from the great city of Florence, were competitors from an early age.

GIOCONDO. It so happened that these two men hated each other bitterly, and would do anything to humiliate the other.

ANSALDO. Well, one day when Ansaldo and his crew ventured beyond the Strait of Gibraltar, they were battered by a furious storm which finally landed them on one of the Canary Islands.

KING. The king of the island welcomed them, and ordered a wonderful feast to be served in a beautiful hall decked with mirrors and gold.

ANSALDO. When it came time to eat, a large group of youths entered the hall carrying strong sticks, and arranged themselves behind the guests. Ansaldo tried to imagine what these youth were about, but could think of no reason for their presence.

RATS. However, all became clear when the food was served, and a horde of huge and ferocious rats poured into the hall and threw themsleves on the meal.

YOUTHS. The youths went wild, attempting to kill the rats or at least to chase them from the room.

ANSALDO. Horrified by the scene before him, Ansaldo sent one of the crew back to the ship.

CREW. When the man returned, he carried a blanket which moved as if alive.

KING. The blanket was brought to the King who opened it to find . . .

ANSALDO. Two cats.

KING. The King, never having laid eyes on such animals before, jumped back in surprise.

ANSALDO. But the cats ran by him excited by the smell of . . .

RATS. Rats. Who were swiftly destroyed by these strange creatures.

ANSALDO. Delighted to repay the King's hospitality,

Ansaldo gave the happy ruler the two cats, which, being one of each sex, were sure to produce a long line of rat-catchers for the people of the island.

KING. The King was overjoyed to have an answer to the rat problem, and to show his gratitude, showered Ansaldo with gold and silver, and emeralds, rubies and diamonds.

ANSALDO. When, after a long journey, Ansaldo returned to Florence, the town was abuzz with the fabulous treasures he brought back from the island. Most people were very happy for this clever sailor . . .

GIOCONDO. Except for Giocondo, who turned a sickly shade of green with envy. He was sure that if that nitwit could weasel a ship full of treasure from those ignorant natives, then he could get at least two ships full. So, acquiring two large schooners and filling them full of the most beautiful and expensive items that Italy had to offer -- silk dresses, velvet pantaloons, pearl-studded leather cloaks -- Giocondo set out for the island.

KING. When he reached the island, the King and all the people were waiting on the shore, hoping that it was their good friend Ansaldo who was returning. However, being a polite people, they tried to hide their disappointment when Giocondo disembarked from the lead ship.

GIOCONDO. Giocondo, wading onto the beach in his most splendid outfit, suitably impressed the backward natives with his dignity.

PEOPLE. When the strange men in the funny clothes sloshed out of the water, no one, not even the children laughed at him.

GIOCONDO. Approaching the King, Giocondo bowed, and ordered his crew to bring forward all the beautiful and expensive gifts he had brought from across the sea. The King was suitably impressed.

KING. The gifts seemed to consist mainly of clothing which the King found an amusing concept.

KING. The gifts could barely supress his joy at these wonderful items which Giocondo referred to as his country's most precious gifts.

KING. The funny little man truly seemed to be sincere, so the King invited him to a feast where Giocondo would be given the island people's most precious gifts in return.

GIOCONDO. When the time for the feast arrived, Giocondo, with visions of gold and silver, and emeralds, rubies and diamonds dancing in his head, sat joyfully to await the conclusion of the meal.

PEOPLE. At the end of the meal, the King brought Giocondo before the people and said . . .

KING. My friend, you come to us from far away to share with us your most precious possessions. We, also, would like you to share in our most precious possessions.

GIOCONDO. At that moment, a youth stepped forward, carrying a beautiful pillow on which sat . . .

ANSALDO. Two tiny kittens.

KING. A male and a female from the first litter of the great animals given to us by your countryman . . .

GIOCONDO. Ansaldo! But, but . . . blustered the enraged Giocondo.

KING. No thanks are necessary among friends, said the King.

PEOPLE. And the funny little man was so moved by the King's generosity, that he could not speak, but ran from the feasting hall to his ship.

KING. The next morning the ships were gone.

GIOCONDO. When the story of Giocondo's folly reached

GIVE AND TAKE

Florence, he became the laughing stock of the city.

ANSALDO. Most of his friends shunned him, but Ansaldo, feeling pity for his old competitor, invited Giocondo to his home for a feast . . .

GIOCONDO. But Giocondo, thinking that Ansaldo was trying to humiliate him further refused to leave the house.

ANSALDO. Sad to say, the poor man never left his house again.

GIOCONDO. He barred the door, and spent the rest of his life imprisoned in his home . . .

ANSALDO. His only company . . .

GIOCONDO. The two cats given to him by the King.

ANSALDO. And in time they became Giocondo's . . .

GIOCONDO. Most precious possession.

STORYTELLERS.

Make no mistake.
There are people who give
And people who take.

> A STORYTELLER. From South America . . .
> STORYTELLERS. LAZY PETER AND THE HAT!

(The following story should be told in pantomime. A selection of appropriate Latin and South American music can be used for background.)

1. The rich FARMER is stockpiling the money he earns from selling livestock.

2. Lazy PETER enters, and seeing the money, makes an unsuccessful attempt to steal it.

3. He then comes up with a plan to trick the farmer out of his money.

4. He takes one small bundle of gold, and bringing it to the BUTCHER, indicates that the butcher should return it to him when he places the tassle of his cap over his right shoulder.

5. He brings a second small bundle of gold to the DOCTOR and indicates that the doctor should return it to him when he places the tassle of his hat over his left shoulder.

6. He brings a third small bundle of gold to the PRIEST and indicates that the priest should return it to him when he places the tassle of his hat over his face.

7. PETER then sidles up to the rich FARMER and makes a big production out of worshipping his hat. When the farmer looks confused, Peter indicates that the hat is magic. The farmer disbelieves him, so Peter takes him to the butcher who gives him a bundle of gold when he moves the tassle of his hat to his right shoulder.

8. Now the FARMER is interested in the hat. He offers to purchase it, and, after pretending to think about it for a while, PETER refuses. The farmer seems resigned until Peter leads him to the DOCTOR, who upon seeing Peter move his tassle to the left side, returns his bundle of gold.

9. Now the FARMER is desperate to have the hat, and PETER, after much coaxing agrees to sell it to him. But the farmer suddenly becomes suspicious. So Peter, huffs off to the PRIEST with the farmer following. When Peter places the

tassle over his face, the priest hands him his bag of gold.

10. Now the FARMER is convinced beyond a shadow of a doubt and pleads with PETER for the hat. Peter refuses until the farmer offers all of his gold, his horse, and finally, his DAUGHTER. His daughter is furious to be sold. Reluctantly, Peter agrees, and after loading all of the gold and the daughter on the horse, tosses the hat to the farmer and pretends to ride off. Secretly, he and the daughter hide and watch the following action.

11. The FARMER rushes to the BUTCHER, but no matter what strange things he does to the hat, the butcher merely looks at him like he's crazy.

12. Beginning to panic, the FARMER rushes to the DOCTOR and gets the same results.

13. Almost hysterical now, he goes to the PRIEST who thinks he's crazy. Finally, foaming with frustration, the FARMER attacks the priest.

14. As the POLICE arrive to arrest the FARMER, PETER and the DAUGHTER emerge from hiding. The farmer demands that Peter be arrested and that all his goods be returned. It looks bad for Peter until the daughter comes to his aid and swears that the farmer gave all the goods as a dowry.

15. The POLICE believe her. Her father is carted off, and she and a very reluctant PETER are married by the PRIEST as the BUTCHER and the DOCTOR look on.

STORYTELLERS.
Make no mistake.
There are people who give
And people who take.

STORYTELLER. A Native American story.
STORYTELLERS. THE LEGEND OF THE BLUEBONNETS! (*Lines prefaced by a "-" should be assigned to individual speakers. Lines prefaced by a "*" should be spoken by the group. You might like to try this as a choral piece with only SHE-WHO-IS-ALONE moving until near the end of the story when they all gather around her.*)

- Back,
- back,
- back in time,
* long ago,
- before the first white person set foot on this continent.
- the people called Comanchee lived and hunted in the southwestern corner of what is now the United States.
- They moved over the countryside, assembling their tipis where the supply of water and buffalo were plentiful.
- But there came a time when a great drought visited the land,
- drying up the streams,
- destroying the grass on which the buffalo fed,
- until finally,
- there was little water,
- sparse vegetation,
- no buffalo.
* It was a time of famine.
- A time of death.
- The first to die were the sick and the weak.

- Next, the old people died.
- Then many, many of the children.
- Before long, there was not a tipi in the village where death had not stopped.
- One child who did survive was
* She-Who-Is-Alone,
- named such by her people because only she of all her family still lived.
- Without mother or father,
- uncle or aunt,
- brother or sister,
* she lived alone.
- Her only companion was a doll,
- a doll of cloth and feathers from the bluejay,
- a doll made by her mother before she died.
- The doll became her mother and father,
- uncle and aunt,
- brother and sister.
* Time passed, but still the drought remained,
- and still the famine fed on the blood of the Comanche people.
- The Shaman said,
- let us dance the dance of the rain to beg the Great Spirits for relief.
- And one man responded,
- But we are weak from lack of food. What kind of dance could we offer?
- And the Shaman replied,
- The dance of those who dance though weak, is a dance that the Great Spirits smile upon.
* So they danced.
- For three days they danced 'til they could dance no more.

54 GIVE AND TAKE

* Only She-Who-Is-Alone kept dancing.
- But the Spirits did not smile.
- The rain did not fall.
- Next, the Shaman said,
- Let us sing the song of the rain to beg the Great Spirits for relief.
- And one woman responded,
- But our throats are dry from lack of water. What kind of song could we offer?
- And the Shaman replied,
- The song of those who sing though their throats are dry, is the song that the Great Spirits will smile upon.
* So they sang.
- For three days they sung until they could sing no more.
* Only She-Who-Is-Alone kept singing.
- But the Spirits did not smile.
* And the rain did not fall.
- And the people huddled together in despair.
* Only She-Who-Is-Alone remained apart,
- clutching the doll that was her family.
- And the Shaman said,
- I will climb to the top of the mountain to beg the Great Spirits for relief.
- And a warrior responded,
- But you are too weary from dancing and singing to climb to the top of the mountain.
- And the Shaman replied,
- It is the attempt of those too weary to try that the Great Spirits will smile upon.
* And he left them.
- For three days he was gone.
- On the third day, the people saw him in the distance,

GIVE AND TAKE

   crawling towards the village.
* They ran to him.
- Did you speak to the Spirits?
- What did they say?
- Tell us Shaman, is there hope?
- The people gathered around him.
* Only She-Who-Is-Alone remained apart.
- And the Shaman said,
- I spoke to the Spirits and the Spirits answered:
* We have given you water, and you drink. We have given you buffalo, and you eat. Everything we have given, you take, but nothing have *you* given back to the water, to the buffalo, to us.
- And the Shaman said,
- I asked them, what must we give? And they replied:
* You must give what you'd most hate to part with.
- But what do we have of value? asked the people.
- Surely, they wouldn't want my beautiful cooking pot. There's no food to cook,
- said one woman as she hurried to her tipi.
* One by one the people left.
- Even the Shaman, discouraged by the selfishness of his people, retired to his tipi.
* Only She-Who-Is-Alone remained,
- cradling the doll that was her family.

- The sun set.
- The stars came out.
- The moon rose.
- The people called Comanche slept the sleep of the hungry.
* Only She-Who-Is-Alone was awake.
- She walked to the campfire, and taking a blazing stick,

carried it to the mountain of the Spirits.
- The fire in one hand,
- the doll in the other,
- she climbed.
- She climbed.
* She climbed all night.
- An hour before dawn, she reached the top of the mountain.
- She gathered twigs and branches, and arranged them in a small circle.
- She placed her doll in the center of the circle.
- She touched the blazing stick to the twigs.
- The dry twigs burst into flames, consuming the doll.

- When the fire had gone out, she took the ashes and cast them
- to the east,
- to the west,
- to the north,
- to the south.
* Then, She-Who-Is-Alone lay down and slept.
- The moon went down.
- The stars went out.
- The sun rose.
* She-Who-Is-Alone awakened.
- She looked to the east,
- to the west,
- to the north,
- to the south,
- and everywhere she looked, she saw beautiful blue flowers where before there had been only parched, dry earth.
- Then the people of the village came clambering up the mountain to behold the miracle of the delicate blue flowers.

GIVE AND TAKE

* The Shaman looked to She-Who-Is-Alone and saw that the doll was gone.
- He said,
- She-Who-Is-Alone has offered freely that which she most cherished, and the Great Spirits, at last, have smiled upon us.
- At that moment, it began to rain.
* And the villagers ran to She-Who-Is-Alone and gave her praise and gratitude.
- It continued to rain.
- And from that day, they called her
* She-Who-Loves-Her-People.
- And still it rained,
- and rained,
- and rained.

STORYTELLERS.
Yes, there's a common thread, a common need –
A well of generosity, a bucket of greed.
Yes, there's a common choice for everybody who lives
Are you a person who takes
Or a person who gives?
Are you a person who takes
Or a person who gives?

(The actors move off the stage chanting the last two lines.)

CURTAIN

A NOTE ON PRODUCTION STYLE

Music

The use of music generated by rhythm instruments and the actors' voices will be most helpful in establishing particular cultures. These rhythms will also provide a means to move from story to story.

Costumes

Actors might wear a basic storyteller's costume to which pieces (*masks, etc.*) could be added for particular stories.

Setting

An empty space with a few boxes and a ladder proved sufficient to our needs.

Props

We found it effective to mime most props. However, a particular "real" prop (*such as Nanabozo's blanket*) might be used to make a cultural point.

Also by
Michael Scanlan...

Candid

A Double Dose

Fortress

Inside / Out

Loose Connections

Out of Control

Something Different

Please visit our website **bakersplays.com** for complete descriptions and licensing information.

www.ingramcontent.com/pod-product-compliance
Lightning Source LLC
Chambersburg PA
CBHW071844290426
44109CB00017B/1916